Moments Of Thought: Trust In God's Guidance

Pastor Jaylon Calhoun

Moments Of Thought: Trust In God's Guidance

© 2024 Dr. Tish Shearer

Book Cover Design: Pastor Jaylon Calhoun

Editor: Dr. Tish Shearer

ALL RIGHTS RESERVED. No part of this book may be reproduced in any written, electronic, recording, or photocopying without written permission of the publisher or author. The exception would be in the case of brief quotations embodied in critical articles or reviews and pages where the publisher or author expressly grants permission.

LEGAL DISCLAIMER. Although the author has made every effort to ensure that the information in this book was correct at press time, the author does not assume hereby disclaim any liability to any party for loss, damage, or disruption caused by errors or omissions, whether such errors or omissions result from negligence, accident, or any other cause.

Published By: Fervently Creations Incorporated

ISBN: 979-889504143-7

PRINTED IN THE UNITED STATES OF AMERICA

Acknowledgments

First and foremost, I give all glory and honor to God, whose guidance and grace have been the foundation of this book. Without His wisdom and inspiration, none of this would have been possible. To my beloved family, thank you for your unwavering support and love. To my wife, your encouragement, patience, and prayers have been my strength. To my children, you are a constant source of joy and inspiration.

To my Anointed Radio Network family, your faith and dedication to our shared mission have been a constant encouragement. Thank you for your prayers, support, and for allowing me the privilege to serve as your leader. To the incredible team at Ferverly Creation Book Publishing thank you for believing in this project and for your expertise in bringing this book to life. Your hard work and dedication are deeply appreciated.

To my dear friends and mentors, thank you for your wise counsel, prayers, and for walking this journey of faith with me. Your impact on my life and ministry is immeasurable. Special thanks to my wife, my children, my sister Jazzman, and Dr. Tish Shearer. Your insights, feedback, and hard work have greatly enriched this book.

Lastly, to the readers of "Moments of Thought: Trust In God's Guidance," thank you for allowing me to share this journey with you. My prayer is that this book will be a source of encouragement and inspiration as you trust in God's guidance and grow in your faith.

In His Service,

Pastor Jaylon Calhoun

TABLE OF CONTENT

FOREWORD	6
FOREWORD	11
CHAPTER 1: WHICH PATH WILL YOU CHOOSE?	13
CHAPTER 2: OVERTHINKING CAUSES UNNECESSARY SIN	19
CHAPTER 3: BEING THE CHURCH	25
CHAPTER 4: ARE YOU IN NEUTRAL?	33
CHAPTER 5: WHAT ARE YOUR PRIORITIES?	39
CHAPTER 6: DO YOU KNOW WHO IS REALLY IN YOUR CORNER?	46
CHAPTER 7: TERMINATORS	54
CHAPTER 8: GOD GIVES YOU STATUS	62
CHAPTER 9: KEEPING IT REAL WITH GOD	69
CHAPTER 10: PLANNED OUT EVIL	79

CHAPTER 11: GOD CALLED YOU	85
CHAPTER 12: NEW BEGINNINGS	93
CHAPTER 13: DISCIPLESHIP	101
CHAPTER 14: LETTING SIN STOP YOUR GROWTH AND DECISIONS	108
CHAPTER 15: THE WORD LOVE WILL MAKE YOU THINK YOU ARE DOING RIGHT	113
CHAPTER 16: SIN HAS THE SAME OUTCOME	117

Foreword

In a day and age that is marked by uncertainty and incessant change, the idea of trusting in proven, divine guidance resonates in a most powerful way than ever before. The timing and release of Jaylon Calhoun's newest literary masterpiece, entitled, "Trusting God's Guidance", is prophetic and necessary for such a time as this. The book emerges at precisely the right moment providing hope, knowledge and wisdom for those that are navigating the turbulent ebbs and flow of this life. As someone that has dedicated decades of my life to studying and teaching theology, spiritual discipline and God's order, I can without hesitation affirm the indelible mark this book will have on its readers and the concise direction it will provide.

For the honorable time I've known Jaylon, what I admire most about him is his ability to be extremely practical with no compromise for scriptural exegesis and integrity. Though his approach is scholarly, it's yet accessible, making complex theological concepts understandable. This results in one of the book's major strengths being its balance between theory and practice. Jaylon masterfully interweaves the spiritual with the pragmatic, ensuring that the readers not only understand the principles of divine guidance, but more importantly its implementation for everyday life.

Jaylon has crafted a work that is both timeless and timely, addressing the perennial need for divine direction while also speaking to our unique present-day challenges and providing a guide for self-development in the process. This book will undoubtedly become a cherished companion for anyone seeking to navigate life's complexities with faith and confidence in God.

Please understand, this book is more than just a collection of inspirational axioms and thoughts but is rather a well-crafted roadmap for anyone seeking specific knowledge about learning to trust the guidance of God. From the beginning chapter entitled, "Which Path Will You Choose" to the chapter entitled, "Terminators", the book is structured in a way that guides the reader through a progressive journey of reflection, inspection, correction, inspiration, motivation, illumination and revelation. This structure also highlights another note-worthy feature of this book, which is its inclusivity. Jaylon understands that the journey to trusting God on this wise is one of faith that is unique and distinctively different for everyone. Whether you are a seasoned Believer or someone exploring this subject for the first time, "Trusting God's Guidance" will provide enriching lessons and encouragement, tailored to your specific need.

The Bible provides us this instruction in Proverbs 3:5-6 (KJV) "Trust in the LORD with all thine heart; and lean not unto thine own understanding. In all thy ways acknowledge him, and he shall direct thy paths." While this scripture is often quoted and used to provide direction, it also can leave the lingering query of, what does this look like in everyday life? How do you literally trust in an invisible God for life's very visible, tangible obstacles and challenges? This book solves this dilemma and as you turn the pages of "Trusting God's Guidance", you find yourself not only gaining insight into God's will for your life, but also experiencing a profound sense of peace and assurance. Jaylon's words, through the anointing of the Holy Spirit, have the power to illuminate your path, helping you identify and embrace divine guidance that is readily and perpetually available to you.

In conclusion, I wholeheartedly endorse "Trusting God's Guidance" and encourage you to delve into its pages with an open heart and mind. Jaylon's wisdom, compassion, and unwavering faith are sure to inspire and guide you, offering a source of strength and encouragement in your spiritual journey. This book is a must-read for anyone seeking to deepen their trust in God's plan and live a life guided by divine wisdom. I encourage you to pray before reading this book and allow the Holy Spirit to open your heart to the places this book will touch in your life. Books of this nature are not written to only make you feel good, no they go to the core of your being and psyche for maximum impact and education.

While the Bible remains our primary theological, education and inspirational guide, every so often, a book comes along that is a note-worthy companion of scripture to enhance our study, guide our focus and ensure we maximize our walk with Christ. "Trusting God's Guidance" is such that note-worthy guide. Embark on this amazing journey with Jaylon Calhoun and discover the transformative power of trusting in God's guidance. It will alter your life in the most positive, powerful and productive way possible.

Pastor Larry Weathers

Foreword

Check out this incredible book that's filled with life-changing principles. Each chapter is packed with wisdom that's all about aligning yourself with God's perfect will. It's the perfect guide for anyone feeling a bit lost and not sure where to begin.

Start with chapter one, "Which Path Will You Choose," and make the declaration, "As for this house, we will serve the Lord." Once you do this, you'll have a clear mission and can start planning your journey accordingly.

Chapter 5, "Figure out Your Priorities," will give you the tools to identify what's essential for nourishing your journey.
As you make progress, make a stop for "gas" in chapter 11, "God Called You." This chapter will refuel you and keep you pushing forward. If you're unsure about what the end goal is, chapter 16, "Sin has the same outcome," will provide the answers.

MOMENTS OF THOUGHTS DURING MY CHRISTIAN WALK

This book is an amazing resource for both new believers and those who may have lost their way. It can be read in any order and still bring you profound insights and revelations.

I pray that God meets you where you are and aligns you with His perfect will. May the reader receive a life-changing revelation and clear instructions directly from the Lord. In Jesus' name, Amen.

Jazzman Brown

Chapter 1: Which Path Will You Choose?

Trust is a concept often discussed in various contexts, but what does it really mean to trust in someone or something? As the Bible verse Proverbs 3:5 reminds us, we are called to trust the Lord with all our hearts and not depend on our own understanding. This is easier said than done, as we often struggle to trust God when faced with uncertainty and fear.

However, as we examine what it truly means to trust in the Lord, we begin to understand that it is an act of faith and surrendering our control to Him. Trusting in God means acknowledging that He knows what is best for us and that we should seek His guidance in making important decisions. This doesn't mean that we should not use our own intelligence and make wise decisions, but it does mean that we should not depend solely on our own understanding.

One way we can learn to trust in God is by listening to His voice. Psalm 119:105 reminds us that the Word of God is a lamp to our feet and a light to our path. This means that as we read the Bible and seek God's guidance through prayer, we can trust that He will lead us in the right direction.

However, it's important to note that we must learn to discern God's voice amidst the noise of the world around us. John 10:27 tells us that God's sheep recognize His voice, but this requires us to cultivate a relationship with Him and learn to listen to His voice through the Holy Spirit.

Trusting in God requires us to focus on Him, not the world's distractions. As Psalm 37:5 reminds us, we must commit our way to the Lord and trust in Him, knowing that He will act on our behalf. This means that we should not be discouraged by the challenges we face but instead trust that God will provide a way.
We should also remember that God sees the whole picture from beginning to end. When we trust in Him, we can be

sure that He knows what is best for us and will guide us accordingly. This can give us peace and confidence in our decision-making.

Trusting in God requires courage, especially when we are faced with difficult decisions or uncertain outcomes. As Isaiah 12:2 reminds us, we should not be afraid but trust in God's strength and salvation. This means that we should stand firm on God's word, even when it goes against the norms of the world around us.
We must also remember that God will not put us in situations that we cannot bear. He will provide us with the courage and strength we need to face any challenge that comes our way.

Trusting in God is not always easy, but it is necessary if we want to live a life of faith and purpose. We must learn to listen to God's voice, focus on Him, and have courage in our God. As we do so, we can trust that He will lead us on the path He has set before us, even if it seems uncertain or difficult.

So, as we go forth in life, let us remember God's faithfulness and trust in His guidance. He is the same God who brought the Israelites out of Egypt and into the Promised Land, and He will do the same for us if we put our trust in Him.

<u>Prayer:</u>
Heavenly Father,

As we embark on this journey through the pages of Chapter 1: "Which Path Will You Choose?" in this book, we come before You with open hearts and minds, seeking Your wisdom and guidance.

Lord, in a world filled with uncertainty and fear, help us to truly understand the depth of what it means to trust in You. Your Word in Proverbs 3:5 instructs us to trust in You with all our hearts and not lean on our understanding. Grant us the grace to surrender control to You, acknowledging that Your ways are higher than ours.

Teach us, O Lord, to discern Your voice amidst the world's noise. May Your Word be a lamp unto our feet and a light unto our path, guiding us in every decision we make. Help us to cultivate a deeper relationship with You, so that we may recognize Your voice through the gentle whisper of the Holy Spirit.

In moments of doubt and difficulty, give us the courage to stand firm in Your promises. For Your Word assures us in Isaiah 12:2 that we need not be afraid, for You are our strength and salvation. Strengthen our faith, Lord, that we may trust in Your provision and guidance, even when the path ahead seems uncertain.

Lord, we acknowledge that trusting in You is not always easy, but it is necessary for a life of faith and purpose. Just as You led the Israelites out of Egypt and into the Promised Land, we trust that You will lead us on the path You have set before us.

As we turn the pages of this chapter and navigate the chapters of our lives, may Your faithfulness be our anchor. May we never waver in our trust in You, knowing that You are with us every step of the way.

MOMENTS OF THOUGHTS DURING MY CHRISTIAN WALK

In Jesus name, we pray,
Amen.

Chapter 2: Overthinking Causes Unnecessary Sin

Overthinking can be a dangerous habit, especially for those seeking to live according to God's will. As the Bible says in James 1:8, "Their loyalty is divided between God and the world, and they are unstable in everything they do." When we overthink, we divide our minds, which can lead to unnecessary sin and confusion.

In this chapter, we will explore the various ways that overthinking can lead to unnecessary sin and how we can overcome this habit by focusing on God and His Word.

1. The Definition Of Confusion

Before we discuss overthinking, it's important to understand the confusion and how it can affect our lives. The Webster dictionary defines confusion as "a state or situation in which many things are happening in a way that is not controlled or orderly." In the Bible, confusion is described as mixing or blending things so they cannot be distinguished.

Satan is the author of confusion, as we see in 1 Corinthians 14:33, "For God is not the author of confusion, but of peace, as in all churches of the saints." When we allow our minds to become confused and divided, we give Satan a foothold in our lives, which can lead to sin and destruction.

Confusion can hinder our progress and growth in our walk with God. It can tear down God's work because nothing gets done. For example, stagnant water can't filter if it doesn't move. Similarly, when we are confused, we can't move forward in our spiritual journey and remain in the same predictable place.

2. Identifying Yourself In Who We Are In Christ

To overcome overthinking and confusion, we must identify ourselves in Christ. We must understand our assignment and how we can grow in our relationship with Him. Knowing God's plan for us makes it easier to stay on track and avoid unnecessary sin.

It's important to reflect on our weaknesses and to seek help and support from our brothers and sisters in Christ. We must be people of our word and promises, just like God, and be able to stand by our commitments. This Christian journey is about discipline; we must stay disciplined in our thoughts and actions.

We must also be careful about who we surround ourselves with. Proverbs 17:4 says, "The wicked enjoy fellowship with others who are wicked; liars enjoy liars." We must surround ourselves with people who will uplift us and not bring us down or tempt us into old habits.

3. Focus On God

Ultimately, focusing on God is the key to overcoming overthinking and confusion. We must understand who we serve and honor Him with our bodies. As 1 Timothy 1:7 says, "For God has not given us a spirit of fear and timidity, but of power, love, and self-discipline."
We are empowered to overcome obstacles and sin when we focus on God and His Word. We can cover more ground going in one direction than going in two at the

same time. As born-again Christians, we must remember that we should never jump back into the mud of sin deliberately. Once Christ has forgiven us and we are clean in His eyes, we must stay disciplined in our thoughts and actions.

In conclusion, overthinking can lead to unnecessary sin and confusion, but we can overcome this habit by focusing on God and His Word. We must identify the confusion in our lives and seek to overcome it with the help of God and our brothers and sisters in Christ. By staying disciplined in our thoughts and actions, we can stay on track with God's plan for our lives.
Proverbs 3:5-6 sums it up perfectly: "Trust in the Lord with all thine heart; and lean not unto thine own understanding. In all thy ways acknowledge him, and he shall direct thy paths."

Prayer:

Heavenly Father,

As we delve into the pages of Chapter 2: "Overthinking Causes Unnecessary Sin" in this book, we come before You seeking Your guidance and wisdom.

Lord, we acknowledge the dangers of overthinking. As James 1:8 warns, it divides our loyalty between You and the world, making us unstable in all our ways. Help us recognize the confusion it brings into our lives, for You are not the author of confusion but of peace.
Grant us clarity of mind, Lord, as we seek to understand who we are in Christ. May we anchor our identities in You, knowing our assignments and growing in our relationship with You. Strengthen us to stand by our commitments and to seek support from our fellow believers, surrounding ourselves with those who uplift and encourage us in our faith journey.

Lord, help us to focus on You above all else. Empower us with Your Spirit, which is not of fear but of power, love, and self-discipline, as 1 Timothy 1:7 reminds us. Guide us to walk in the direction You have set before us, avoiding the pitfalls of overthinking and unnecessary sin.

As we conclude this chapter, may we hold fast to the wisdom of Proverbs 3:5-6, trusting in You with all our hearts and leaning not on our own understanding. Direct our paths, O Lord, as we strive to overcome overthinking and confusion, and to live according to Your will.

In Jesus name, we pray,
Amen.

Chapter 3: Being the Church

When we hear the word "church," we often think of a physical building where people gather to worship God. But being the church is more than just attending a church service. It is about embodying the principles of God and living them out in our daily lives. The Bible tells us in Ephesians 3:16-17, "that He would grant you, according to the riches of His glory, to be strengthened with might through His Spirit in the inner man, that Christ may dwell in your hearts through faith; that you, being rooted and grounded in love." This verse shows us that being in the church means having Christ dwell in our hearts through faith and being rooted and grounded in love. In this chapter, we will explore three principles that we should hold as we strive to be the church.

First Point: Accountability

The first principle we should hold as we strive to be the church is accountability. In Ephesians 4:25, the Bible tells us, "Therefore, laying aside falsehood, SPEAK TRUTH EACH ONE of you WITH HIS NEIGHBOR, for we are members of one another." This verse reminds us that we are all members of one body and, therefore, should hold each other accountable. It is essential to remember that at all times, regardless of where we are, we should be holding ourselves accountable to God in our way of life and our decisions.

In Ephesians 4:15-16, the Bible further emphasizes the importance of accountability by stating, "but speaking the truth in love, we are to grow up in all aspects into Him who is the head, even Christ, from whom the whole body, being fitted and held together by what every joint supplies, according to the proper working of each individual part, causes the growth of the body for the building up of itself in love." This verse highlights that speaking the truth in love is essential to the growth and building up of the body of Christ. When we hold each other accountable, we help each other grow in our faith and become better followers of Christ.

Second Point: Relationship

The second principle we should hold as we strive to be the church is a relationship. As Christians, after holding each other accountable, we must know how to maintain a relationship with the body of Christ and with God. This means that we should communicate and try to understand each other even when we disagree. In 1 Corinthians 12:25-26, the Bible states, "so that there may be no division in the body, but that the members may have the same care for one another. And if one member suffers, all the members suffer with it; if one member is honored, all the members rejoice with it." This verse emphasizes that we are all one body and that we should care for each other as we would care for ourselves.

In Ephesians 5:29-30, the Bible further emphasizes the importance of relationships in the body of Christ by stating, "for no one ever hated his own flesh, but nourishes and cherishes it, just as Christ also does the church because we are members of His body." This verse reminds us that we are all members of the body of Christ, and we should, therefore, nourish and cherish each other.

Remembering that our relationships with each other and God are crucial to our growth and development as believers is essential.

Third Point: Seeking God's Knowledge

The third principle we should hold as we strive to be the church is seeking God's knowledge. There are many false prophets today, and it is essential to know the Bible for ourselves. We need to know whether what people say about God is true or not. Churches are not teaching the Bible as much as they used to do. Many churches focus more on entertaining and making church fun and interesting rather than teaching the Word of God. Sunday schools are not teaching Bible stories; they have cartoon stories with good moral truths. However, eternal life is too important to let it be up to someone else to teach us. We have the Bible, which we need to read for ourselves. We need to take the time to study it and learn. We really do not have an excuse not to know the truth.

In 1 Timothy 2:1-4, the Bible encourages us to pray and

intercede for all people, including kings and those in high positions. It also states that God desires all people to be saved and come to know the truth. Seeking God's knowledge is critical to our spiritual growth and development, and reading the Bible every day is essential. We should have a set time to read and meditate on God's Word each day. We should pray and ask God to help us understand and remember what we read. Memorizing important verses and reviewing them often will help us keep them fresh in our minds.

False teachers should not fool us; instead, we should know the truth for ourselves. The Bible is our guidebook, and we should use it to navigate life's challenges. We must not rely solely on the teachings of others but seek to understand and interpret the Bible's truth for ourselves.

In conclusion, being in the church is more than just attending a church service. It is about embodying God's principles and living them out in our daily lives. We should hold each other accountable, maintain relationships with the body of Christ and with God, and seek God's knowledge. These three principles are crucial to our growth and development as believers and help us be effective witnesses of Christ to the world.

We need to prepare for the spiritual battle we face daily, and the only way we can conquer our trials and storms is by putting on the whole armor of God. Ephesians 6:10-17 describes the whole armor of God, which includes having our loins girt about with truth, the breastplate of righteousness, feet shod with the preparation of the gospel of peace, the shield of faith, the helmet of salvation, and the sword of the Spirit, which is the Word of God.

Our help comes from staying close to the body of Christ and constantly praying to God, and our knowledge and help come from staying in the Word. Let us strive to be the church, not just go to church and live out God's principles daily, becoming effective witnesses of Christ to the world.

Prayers:

MOMENTS OF THOUGHTS DURING MY CHRISTIAN WALK

Heavenly Father,

As we explore Chapter 3: "Being the Church" in this book, we come before You with hearts open to receive Your wisdom and guidance.

Lord, help us to understand that being the church goes beyond mere attendance at a physical building; it is about embodying Your principles and living them out daily. Grant us the strength, Lord, to be rooted and grounded in love, with Christ dwelling in our hearts through faith.

Teach us, O Lord, the importance of accountability within the body of Christ. May we speak the truth in love, helping one another grow and build up the body of Christ. Help us to hold each other accountable, always striving to live lives that honor You.

Lord, deepen our relationships within the body of Christ and with You. May we care for one another as members of the same body, rejoicing in each other's victories and sharing in each other's sorrows. Help us nourish and cherish one another, reflecting Christ has love for His church.

Guide us, Lord, in seeking Your knowledge. In a world filled with misinformation and false teachings, help us to be grounded in Your Word. Grant us the discipline to study Your Word daily, to pray without ceasing, and to seek Your truth above all else. Protect us from the deceit of false teachers and empower us to discern truth from falsehood.

As we conclude this chapter, may we be equipped with the whole armor of God, ready to face the spiritual battles we encounter each day. Strengthen us, Lord, to be effective witnesses of Christ to the world, living out Your principles in our daily lives.

In Jesus name, we pray,
Amen.

Chapter 4: Are You in Neutral?

Are you in neutral? This question is one that we should all ask ourselves. It is easy to become complacent in our walk with God and forget the call that He has placed on our lives. Like many of us, Jonah was a prophet who found himself in a place of disobedience to God's calling. However, God did not abandon Jonah, but instead used his disobedience to bring about His will.

This chapter will explore Jonah's story and the lessons we can learn from it. We will also look at the concept of predestination versus free will and how it relates to our Christian journey. Finally, we will discuss the importance of staying active in our walk with God and the consequences of being neutral.

Jonah's Story:

Jonah was a prophet who God gave a message to preach

to the people of Nineveh. Instead of obeying God's call, Jonah chose to run away. He boarded a ship and sailed in the opposite direction. God sent a storm that threatened to destroy the ship, and the sailors cast lots to determine who was responsible. The lot fell on Jonah, who confessed to the sailors that he was running away from God. The sailors threw Jonah into the sea, and a large fish swallowed him.

While inside the fish, Jonah prayed to God, and God heard his cry. Jonah acknowledged his disobedience and asked for forgiveness. God commanded the fish to vomit Jonah onto dry land, and Jonah went to Nineveh to preach God's message. The people of Nineveh repented, and God spared the city.

Lessons From Jonah's Story:

Disobedience Has Consequences.

Jonah's story teaches us that disobedience to God's calling has consequences. When we choose to go our own way, we are running away from God and the blessings that He has in store for us. God's plans for our lives are always better than our own, and we should trust in Him and obey His calling.

God's Grace Is Greater Than Our Disobedience.

Despite Jonah's disobedience, God did not abandon him. He used Jonah's disobedience to bring about His will. God's grace is greater than our disobedience, and He can use even our mistakes for His glory.

God Always Makes A Way Of Escape.

When Jonah was in the belly of the fish, he cried out to God, and God heard his cry. God always provides a way of escape. When we face difficult situations, we can cry out to God, who will hear us and provide a way out.

Predestination Vs. Free Will:

The concept of predestination versus free will has been

debated by theologians for centuries. Predestination is the belief that God has predetermined who will be saved and who will be lost. On the other hand, free will is the belief that we can choose whether or not to accept God's gift of salvation.

The Bible contains verses that support both predestination and free will. Jeremiah 1:5 and Galatians 1:15 speak to predestination, while Proverbs 16:9 and 1 Corinthians 10:13 speak to free will. The truth is that both predestination and free will are Biblical concepts, and we should not reject one in favor of the other.

The Importance Of Staying Active:

Staying active in our walk with God is crucial. The Bible tells us that we were once in darkness, but now we are light in the Lord (Ephesians 5:8). We should not revert back to our old ways but should continue to grow in our relationship with God. We should read the Bible, pray, attend church,

Prayer:

Heavenly Father,

As we delve into the pages of Chapter 4: "Are You in Neutral?" in this book, we come before You with humble hearts, seeking Your guidance and wisdom.

Lord, help us examine our hearts and lives honestly, asking ourselves if we are truly aligned with Your will or have become complacent in our walk with You. Just as Jonah found himself in a place of disobedience, remind us that Your call on our lives is not to be ignored or taken lightly.

Teach us, O Lord, the lessons from Jonah's story. Help us to understand that disobedience to Your calling has consequences, but Your grace is greater than our mistakes. Empower us to trust in Your plans for our lives and to obey Your commands without hesitation.

Guide us, Lord, in understanding the concept of

predestination versus free will. Help us to embrace both Biblical truths, recognizing that Your sovereignty does not negate our responsibility to choose obedience. Grant us wisdom to navigate this theological debate with humility and grace.

Lord, keep us active in our walk with You. May we never grow complacent or stagnant in our faith but continue to pursue You fervently and passionately. Strengthen us to read Your Word, pray without ceasing, and regularly fellowship with other believers.

As we conclude this chapter, may we be reminded of Your faithfulness and love. Help us to align our lives with Your will and stay active in our pursuit of You and Your Kingdom.

In Jesus' name, we pray,
Amen.

Chapter 5: What Are Your Priorities?

In life, it is easy to get caught up in the things that seem important in the moment. Whether it is material possessions, personal ambitions, or the opinions of others, we can lose sight of what truly matters. However, if we want to live a fulfilling and purposeful life, it is essential that we take the time to examine our priorities and ensure that they align with our values and beliefs. This chapter will explore the importance of having our priorities in order, using biblical scripture and practical examples to highlight key principles.

Point 1: Fear of God

The fear of God is the foundation of wisdom and the beginning of knowledge (Proverbs 9:10). When we fear God, we acknowledge His power and sovereignty over our lives. We recognize that we are not in control and that we need His guidance and protection. This fear should not be one of terror or dread, but rather a healthy reverence and respect for God and His ways.

Luke 12:29-31 reminds us not to worry about the things of this world, such as what we will eat or drink. Instead, we are called to seek God's kingdom and trust that He will provide for our needs. This does not mean that we should not work hard or plan for the future, but rather that our trust and reliance should be on God, not our own efforts or possessions.

Additionally, we should be willing to pray for protection and change in ourselves. We cannot change ourselves until we want to, and having a fear of God can motivate us to desire change and growth. It is important to live by God's standards rather than our own and to continually seek His guidance and direction in all areas of our lives.

Point 2: Family

Family is a gift from God, and it is our responsibility to care for and support those in our households (2 Timothy

5:8). This includes not only our immediate family but also extended family members and those in our community who are in need. We are called to love and serve one another, putting the needs of others before our own.

Unfortunately, it is easy to get caught up in our own agendas and forget about the needs of those around us. We may hold grudges or let conflicts go unresolved, leading to strained relationships and distance between family members. This can have long-lasting effects and can even cause us to deny the true faith, as mentioned in 2 Timothy 5:8.

Proverbs 10:4 reminds us that diligence and hard work lead to wealth, while laziness leads to poverty. This applies not only to financial wealth but also to the wealth of our relationships and family connections. We must be willing to put in the effort to care for and nurture our family relationships, even when it is difficult or inconvenient.

Point 3: Finance

Money is a powerful force in our society, and it can be easy to become consumed by the desire for wealth and material possessions. However, as Ecclesiastes 5:10 reminds us, the pursuit of money is ultimately meaningless. It will never bring true fulfillment or happiness.

Hebrews 13:5 instructs us to be content with what we have and to avoid the love of money. This does not mean that we cannot enjoy the blessings and resources that God has given us, but rather that we should not make them the focus of our lives. We should be willing to give generously to others and to use our resources for the glory of God rather than hoarding them for our own selfish purposes.

Ultimately, our finances should be viewed as a tool for accomplishing God's purposes, rather than an end in themselves. We should seek to use our resources in ways that honor God and further His kingdom rather than pursuing wealth and possessions for their own sake.

In conclusion, having our priorities in order is essential for living a fulfilling and purposeful life. We must recognize the importance of the fear of God, caring for our families, and managing our finances in a way that honors Him. When we put God first in our lives, He will direct us and crown our efforts with success (Proverbs 3:6).

It is easy to get caught up in the busyness and distractions of life, but we must remember that our time on this earth is short. We should strive to live in a way that reflects our values and beliefs and positively impacts those around us. This requires continually re-evaluating our priorities and a willingness to make changes when necessary.

As Ghandi said, "Action expresses priorities." We must take action to ensure that our priorities align with our values and beliefs and that we are living in a way that honors God and brings glory to His name. May we all seek to live lives that reflect His love and grace and bring joy and fulfillment to ourselves and those around us.

Prayer:

Heavenly Father,

As we delve into the pages of Chapter 5: "Where Are Your Priorities?" in this book, we come before You with humble hearts, seeking Your guidance and wisdom.

Lord, help us to examine our priorities honestly and to align them with Your will. Grant us the wisdom to fear You, acknowledging Your sovereignty over our lives and trusting in Your provision. May our fear of You lead us to seek Your kingdom above all else, knowing that You will provide for our needs.

Teach us, O Lord, the importance of family. May we cherish and nurture our relationships, putting the needs of others before our own. Help us to mend broken relationships and to love one another as You have loved us. Strengthen our families, Lord, that they may be a beacon of Your love and grace to the world.

Guide us, Lord, in managing our finances. Help us to be content with what we have and to avoid the love of money. May we use our resources to further Your kingdom and to bless others, rather than pursuing wealth and possessions for their own sake.

Lord, as we conclude this chapter, may our priorities be aligned with Your will. May we seek first Your kingdom and righteousness, knowing that You will add all things unto us. Give us the courage to take action and to live lives that reflect Your love and grace.
In Jesus' name, we pray,
Amen.

Chapter 6: Do You Know Who is Really in Your Corner?

The spiritual gift of discernment is essential in the Body of Christ. It is the ability to distinguish good from evil, truth from lies, and sound doctrine from false teachings. Discernment is the ability to see beyond the surface level and perceive things that others may miss. It is an ability to sense something isn't right, uncover false teachings easily, and have a great hunger for biblical knowledge and teachings.

Hebrews 5:14 states, "But solid food is for the mature, for those who have their powers of discernment trained by constant practice to distinguish good from evil." This verse highlights that spiritual discernment is a skill that needs to be developed through constant practice. Not everyone has this gift, and it is important to understand the biblical standard for spiritual discernment.

Point 1: The Source of Discernment

Solomon was one of the wisest men who ever lived, and he knew where true discernment came from. In 1 Kings 2:9, he asked God, "Give your servant, therefore, an understanding mind to govern your people, that I may discern between good and evil, for who is able to govern this your great people?" God answered Solomon's prayer because he asked for understanding to discern what was right (1 Kings 3:11).

The Psalmist also knew where discernment came from, as he prayed to God in Psalm 119:125, "I am your servant; give me discernment that I may understand your statute." Discernment is a gift from God given to those seeking it. It is not something that can be learned from human wisdom or knowledge.

Any nation that ignores the Word of God cannot have discernment because, as Moses wrote about one such nation, "For they are a nation void of counsel, and there is no understanding in them. If they were wise, they would understand this; they would discern their latter end" (Deuteronomy 32:28-29). The source of discernment is God and His Word.

Point 2: Relationship

Discernment is not limited to spiritual matters; it also applies to relationships. The people we surround ourselves with have a significant impact on our lives. Proverbs 13:20 says, "Whoever walks with the wise becomes wise, but the companion of fools will suffer harm." This verse highlights the importance of choosing wise and discerning friends.

Proverbs 22:24-25 warns, "Make no friendship with a man given to anger, nor go with a wrathful man, lest you learn his ways and entangle yourself in a snare." This verse emphasizes that bad company corrupts good character. We must be careful who we allow to influence us and ensure they align with God's Word.

1 Corinthians 15:33 says, "Do not be deceived: 'Bad company ruins good morals.'" This verse emphasizes that the people we surround ourselves with can affect our behavior and our discernment. We must choose wisely and pray for discernment in our relationships.

Point 3: False Prophets

False prophets are prevalent in today's churches. They infiltrate churches and deceive many people. Jesus warned his disciples in Matthew 7:15, "Beware of false prophets, who come to you in sheep's clothing but inwardly are ravenous wolves." False prophets are deceptive and can appear as an "angel of light."

2 Corinthians 11:3-4 says, "But I fear that somehow your pure and undivided devotion to Christ will be corrupted, just as Eve was deceived by the cunning ways of the serpent. You happily put up with whatever anyone tells you, even if they preach a different Jesus than the one we preach, or a different kind of Spirit than the one you received, or a different kind of gospel than the one you

believed." False prophets twist the truth and lead people astray.

It is important to have discernment when it comes to false prophets. We must compare everything to the Word of God to ensure that it aligns with His teachings. 1 John 4:1 says, "Beloved, do not believe every spirit, but test the spirits to see whether they are from God, for many false prophets have gone out into the world." We must test the spirits and examine their teachings to ensure they align with God's Word.

Hebrews 4:12 says, "For the word of God is living and active, sharper than any two-edged sword, piercing to the division of soul and of spirit, of joints and of marrow, and discerning the thoughts and intentions of the heart." God's Word is the ultimate source of discernment. It can pierce through the deepest parts of our hearts and discern the truth from a lie.

In conclusion, the gift of discernment is essential in the Body of Christ. It is distinguishing good from evil, truth from lies, and sound doctrine from false teachings. Discernment cannot be learned from human wisdom or knowledge but is a gift from God given to those who seek it.

The source of discernment is God and His Word. We must seek His wisdom and discernment in all aspects of our lives, including our relationships and spiritual teachings. We must surround ourselves with wise and discerning friends and test everything against the Word of God to ensure it aligns with His teachings.

False prophets are prevalent in today's churches, and we must have discernment to identify them. We must compare everything to the Word of God to ensure that it aligns with His teachings. The Word of God is the ultimate source of discernment, and it has the power to discern the truth from a lie.

In closing, we must seek God's wisdom and discernment in all aspects of our lives. We must choose our relationships wisely and test everything against the Word of God to ensure it aligns with His teachings. May we continue to seek God's discernment and use it to glorify Him and further His Kingdom.

<u>Prayer:</u>

Heavenly Father,

As we delve into the pages of Chapter 6: "Do You Know Who Is Really in Your Corner?" in this book, we come before You with hearts open to receive Your wisdom and discernment.
Lord, we recognize the importance of the spiritual gift of discernment in the Body of Christ. Grant us, we pray, the ability to distinguish good from evil, truth from lies, and sound doctrine from false teachings. May our discernment be sharpened by constant practice and rooted in Your Word.

Teach us, O Lord, the true source of discernment. Help us to seek Your wisdom and understanding in all aspects of our lives, knowing that You are the ultimate source of truth. Guide us in our relationships so that we may surround ourselves with wise and discerning friends who will lead us closer to You.

Protect us, Lord, from the influence of false prophets. Give us the discernment to test everything against Your Word, ensuring that it aligns with Your teachings. May we not be deceived by those who twist the truth, but remain steadfast in Your Word.

Lord, as we conclude this chapter, may our discernment bring glory to Your name and further Your Kingdom. Help us to use this gift to glorify You and to lead others to the truth. May we continue to seek Your wisdom and discernment in all that we do.
In Jesus' name, we pray,
Amen.

MOMENTS OF THOUGHTS DURING MY CHRISTIAN WALK

Chapter 7: Terminators

The Terminator franchise has been a household name since its inception in 1984 with the release of the first movie. The plot revolves around a post-apocalyptic world where Skynet, an artificial intelligence system, has initiated a nuclear holocaust to wipe out humanity. The only hope for the survival of humanity lies with John Connor, a human resistance leader who fights against Skynet's forces. In this battle for survival, Skynet deploys cyborg assassins known as Terminators to eliminate John Connor and his mother Sarah Connor. The Terminators are programmed to destroy, steal, and kill, as stated in John 10:10 of the Bible. This chapter explores the three points on how the Terminators embody the scriptural teaching of the enemy's tactics to destroy, steal and kill.

Point 1: Destroy You By Your Past Experience

The first Terminator introduced in the franchise is the T-800, played by Arnold Schwarzenegger. The T-800 is a sheer metallic terror wrapped in muscles that never stops until its mission is accomplished. It is virtually unstoppable and can withstand significant damage, making it a formidable opponent. The T-800's mission is to kill Sarah Connor, the mother of John Connor, as Skynet knows that John will lead the resistance against them in the future.

The T-800's approach to killing Sarah Connor embodies the enemy's tactic of destroying individuals by their past experiences. The T-800 is programmed to eliminate Sarah Connor before John Connor is born, as it knows that John's existence poses a threat to Skynet. Similarly, the enemy uses an individual's past experiences to destroy them. The enemy uses our past sins, failures, and disappointments to make us feel unworthy, hopeless, and defeated. The Bible reminds us that we have all sinned and fallen short of God's glory (Romans 3:23) and that we will be hated by all for Christ's sake (Luke 21:17). However, we must not let our past define us and keep us from fulfilling our God-given purpose. Instead, we should seek God's forgiveness and grace, which can free us from the bondage of our past experiences.

Point 2: Steal Your Present Joy

The T-1000 introduced in Terminator Genisys is a new timeline-disrupting cyborg assassin that has a lot in common with its counterpart from Terminator 2: Judgment Day. The T-1000 is made of liquid metal that can take on any form and can mold into an individual's present life to infiltrate it. The T-1000's objective is to kill Sarah Connor and stop John Connor from leading the human resistance.

The T-1000's approach to killing Sarah Connor embodies the enemy's tactic of stealing an individual's present joy. The T-1000 infiltrates Sarah's life by taking on the form of a police officer and tries to deceive her into trusting it. Similarly, the enemy tries to deceive us by molding itself into our present life and stealing our joy. The enemy uses distractions, temptations, and worldly desires to steal our joy and lead us away from God's plan for our lives. The Bible warns us to be sober-minded and watchful because our adversary the devil prowls around like a roaring lion, seeking someone to devour (1 Peter 5:8). We must put to death what is earthly in us, such as sexual immorality, impurity, passion, evil desire, and covetousness, which is idolatry (Colossians 3:5). By focusing on God's plan for our lives, we can resist the enemy's tactics and experience the joy that God has in store for us.

Point 3: Kill Your Future God Had In Store For You

The third Terminator introduced in the franchise is John Connor, played by Jason Clarke in Terminator Genisys. In this movie, John Connor is transformed into a Terminator after being infected by a swarm of tiny nanobots that have slowly replaced all his normal cells. John Connor, now a Terminator, has the same objective as the other Terminators, which is to eliminate Sarah Connor and stop John Connor from leading the human resistance.

John Connor's transformation into a Terminator embodies the enemy's tactic of killing an individual's future that God had in store for them. The enemy wants to kill the future that God has planned for us by tempting us to sin and making us believe that there is no hope for us. The Bible tells us that Jesus Christ is the same yesterday, today, and forever (Hebrews 13:8-9) and warns us not to be led away by diverse and strange teachings. The enemy disguises itself as an angel of light (2 Corinthians 11:14) and tries to lead us astray from God's plan for our lives.

In conclusion, the Terminators in the Terminator franchise embody the scriptural teaching of the enemy's tactics to destroy, steal, and kill. The T-800 embodies the enemy's tactic of destroying individuals by their past experiences. The T-1000 embodies the enemy's tactic of stealing an individual's present joy. John Connor, as a Terminator, embodies the enemy's tactic of killing an individual's future that God had in store for them.

However, the Bible tells us that we can resist the enemy's tactics by staying under the cover of God and focusing on His plan for our lives. As John 16:22 states, "And ye now, therefore, have sorrow: but I will see you again, and your heart shall rejoice, and your joy no man taketh from you." We can take comfort in knowing that God has plans for our welfare and not for evil, to give us a future and hope (Jeremiah 29:11).

Prayer:

Heavenly Father,

As we reflect on the insights shared in Chapter 7: "Terminators," we come before You with hearts open to Your guidance and protection. We recognize the importance of discerning the enemy's tactics to destroy, steal, and kill, as portrayed through the Terminators in the Terminator franchise.

Lord, we see how the T-800, T-1000, and John Connor as a Terminator represent the enemy's strategies to harm Your children. The T-800 seeks to destroy us by exploiting our past experiences, while the T-1000 aims to steal our present joy by deceiving and distracting us. John Connor, as a Terminator, embodies the enemy's desire to kill the future You have planned for us, filling us with doubt and despair.

But we take solace in Your Word, knowing that You have not given us a spirit of fear but of power, love, and a sound mind (2 Timothy 1:7). Help us to discern the enemy's schemes and to stand firm in Your truth. May we find strength in knowing that nothing can separate us from Your love (Romans 8:38-39) and that Your plans for us are for good and not for harm, to give us a future and hope (Jeremiah 29:11).

Lord, protect us from the attacks of the enemy and surround us with Your divine shield of protection. Fill us with Your Holy Spirit, granting us wisdom and discernment to recognize and resist the enemy's lies. Help us to cling to Your promises and to walk in faith, knowing that You are always with us, guiding us and leading us in Your perfect will.

May this chapter serve as a reminder of the importance of staying vigilant and rooted in Your Word. Empower us to overcome the enemy's tactics and to walk confidently in the victory You have already won for us through Jesus Christ.

In His name, we pray,

Amen.

Chapter 8: God Gives You Status

The passage in 1 Samuel 2:8-9 talks about how God raises up the poor from the dust and lifts the needy from the ash heap to make them sit with princes and inherit a seat of honor. This verse is a part of Hannah's prayer, where she asks God for a son, promising to dedicate his life to God. God fulfills her request, and she gives birth to Samuel, who later becomes a great prophet of Israel. This passage is an excellent reminder that God can raise us up from our lowly state and give us a position of honor and influence.

Do You Meet The Standard Of Man?

We often set standards for ourselves based on what society deems as important. We want to be rich, famous, and successful. However, these standards are not always in line with what God wants for us. God's standard is different, and it is focused on our character and our relationship with Him. He wants us to be humble, kind, and faithful. It's essential to remember that God does not look at our outward appearance or our social status but at our hearts.

Do You Meet The Standard Of God?

God's standard for us is different from what society deems as important. He wants us to focus on our character and our relationship with Him. It's not about being rich, famous, or successful, but about being humble, kind, and faithful. When we meet God's standard, we can experience true joy and peace in our lives.

Have You Ever Felt Like You Aren't Qualified For Something?

Many times, we feel like we are not qualified for something that we want to do. It could be a new job, a promotion, or a ministry opportunity. However, God does not call the qualified; He qualifies the called. He gives us the skills, the knowledge, and the resources we need to fulfill the purpose He has for our lives.

Point 1: God Will Build You

In Acts 20:32, Paul commends the believers to God and the word of His grace, which is able to build them up and give them an inheritance among all those who are sanctified. The experiences we go through in life help build us up and give us the tools we need for our future. When we go through difficult times, we may not understand why, but God is using those experiences to shape us into the person He wants us to be.

Point 2: God Will Place You In Places Higher Than Your Standards

Romans 8:30 says that those whom God predestined, He also called, justified, and glorified. In Jeremiah 24:6, God promises to set His eyes on His people for good, build them up, and not tear them down. He will plant them and not uproot them. God places us in places of influence so that we can be a positive influence on others. Just like how He placed Esther as queen, God can also place us in positions of authority and influence.

Psalm 34:15 says that the eyes of the Lord are toward the righteous, and His ears are toward their cry. God is always watching over us, and He hears our cries. Life is short, and everything that happens to us will be a part of our experience. We must focus on God and trust that He will ordain our future and destiny. When we meet His standard, He will raise us up and place us in positions of influence to make a positive impact on the world.

God wants us to be the best versions of ourselves and fulfill His purpose for our lives. We need to trust Him and have faith that He will guide us in the right direction.

When we go through difficult times, it's easy to lose sight of God's plan for our lives. However, we need to remember that God is in control and has a plan for us. We need to trust Him and have faith that He will provide for us and guide us through every situation.

In conclusion, the passage in 1 Samuel 2:8-9 is a beautiful reminder that God can raise us up from our lowly state and give us a position of honor and influence. It's essential to focus on God's standard and not society's standard. When we meet God's standard, He will build us up and place us in positions of influence to make a positive impact on the world. We need to trust God and have faith that He will guide us in the right direction. Life is short, and we need to make the most of it by fulfilling God's purpose for our lives.

Prayer:

Heavenly Father,
As we delve into Chapter 8: "God gives you Status," we are reminded of Your divine power to raise us up from our lowly state and grant us positions of honor and influence. Your Word in 1 Samuel 2:8-9 speaks of Your ability to lift the poor from the dust and elevate the needy from the ash heap, granting them seats of honor among princes. We come before You with hearts full of gratitude for Your grace and mercy.

MOMENTS OF THOUGHTS DURING MY CHRISTIAN WALK

Lord, in a world that often measures worth by material success and societal standards, help us to align our lives with Your standards. May we seek humility, kindness, and faithfulness above worldly riches and fame. Teach us to focus on our character and our relationship with You, knowing that true joy and peace come from meeting Your standard.

When doubts of inadequacy plague our minds, remind us that You do not call the qualified; You qualify the called. Strengthen our faith and equip us with the skills, knowledge, and resources we need to fulfill Your purpose for our lives. Help us to trust in Your provision and to step boldly into the opportunities You place before us.

Lord, as we journey through life's experiences, we trust that You are building us up for our future. Even in the midst of trials and challenges, may we find comfort in knowing that You are shaping us into the people You desire us to be. Grant us the wisdom to discern Your leading and the courage to follow Your path.

Just as You placed Esther as queen and elevated countless others to positions of influence, we trust that You will also place us in places higher than our standards. Help us to steward these positions with integrity and humility, using them as platforms to positively influence those around us.

In times of uncertainty, may we fix our eyes on You, knowing that Your plans for us are for good and not for harm, to give us a future and hope. As we strive to meet Your standard, may Your eyes be upon us, and Your ears attentive to our cries. Guide us, Lord, in fulfilling the purpose You have ordained for our lives.

In Jesus name, we pray,

Amen.

Chapter 9: Keeping It Real With God

Are we living our lives in accordance with the teachings of the Bible or are we simply paying lip service to God? It is important that we keep it real with God by loving Him with all our heart, soul, and mind, and by loving our neighbors as ourselves. The Bible makes it clear that these two commandments are the foundation of all the law and the prophets. When we blur the line between God's way and the world's way, we call evil good and good evil, and we put darkness for light and light for darkness. This deadness to moral distinctions is a sign of deep moral corruption and fully deserves to have a special "woe" pronounced against it.

We need to be careful not to justify the wicked and condemn the just, for both actions are an abomination to the Lord. We should not be wise in our own eyes, for self-conceit is the antithesis of humility. We must fear the Lord and shun evil, seeking true wisdom from God by bringing our understanding into captivity to the obedience of faith.

Keeping it real with God means being honest with ourselves and with Him. It means acknowledging our weaknesses and our need for His grace and mercy. It means living our lives in accordance with His will, not our own. It means being patient, kind, not envious, not boasting, not proud, not dishonoring others, not self-seeking, not easily angered, keeping no record of wrongs, not delighting in evil, rejoicing with the truth, always protecting, always trusting, always hoping, and always persevering.

When we keep it real with God, we will have peace, joy, and fulfillment in our lives. We will be able to love others as ourselves, even those who treat us poorly. We will be able to forgive those who have wronged us, just as God has forgiven us. We will be able to live a life that is pleasing to Him, not because we have to, but because we want to. We will be able to live a life that is a testimony to His grace and mercy, and to the power of His love to transform our lives.

Keeping it real with God also means being authentic in our worship and in our relationship with Him. We should not try to impress others with our spiritual prowess or with how much we know about the Bible. Instead, we should come to God with a humble heart, ready to listen and to learn from Him. We should worship Him in spirit and in truth, not just go through the motions of religious rituals. As Jesus said to the woman at the well in John 4:23-24: "But the hour is coming, and is now here when the true worshipers will worship the Father in spirit and truth, for the Father seeks such as these to worship him. God is spirit, and those who worship him must worship in spirit and truth."

When we keep it real with God, we will experience a deep and meaningful relationship with Him, one that is based on honesty, trust, and love. We will be able to approach Him with confidence, knowing that He hears us and that He cares about us. We will be able to pour out our hearts to Him, sharing our joys and our sorrows, our hopes and our fears. And we will be able to hear His voice, guiding us and directing us along the path that He has for us.

Keeping it real with God also means being honest with ourselves about our sins and our need for His forgiveness. We cannot hide our sins from God, nor can we deceive ourselves into thinking that we are without sin. As the apostle John wrote in 1 John 1:8-10: "If we say that we have no sin, we deceive ourselves, and the truth is not in us. If we confess our sins, he who is faithful and just will forgive us our sins and cleanse us from all unrighteousness. If we say that we have not sinned, we make him a liar, and his word is not in us."

When we confess our sins to God and ask for His forgiveness, He is faithful and just to forgive us and to cleanse us from all unrighteousness. We can then walk in the freedom and the joy that comes from knowing that we are forgiven and that we are loved by God.

In conclusion, keeping it real with God is about living our lives in accordance with His will, not our own. It is about loving Him with all our heart, soul, and mind, and loving our neighbors as ourselves. It is about being authentic in our worship and in our relationship with Him and being honest with ourselves about our sins and our need for His forgiveness. When we keep it real with God, we will experience a deep and meaningful relationship with Him, one that is based on honesty, trust, and love. We will be able to live a life that is pleasing to Him, one that is a testimony to His grace and mercy, and to the power of His love to transform our lives.

One way to keep it real with God is to spend time in prayer and reading the Bible. Through prayer, we can communicate with God and share our hearts with Him. We can ask Him for guidance, strength, and wisdom, and we can thank Him for His blessings and His faithfulness. Reading the Bible helps us understand God's character and His will for our lives. It also helps us grow in our faith and become more like Christ.

Another way to keep it real with God is to be obedient to His commands. As Jesus said in John 14:15, "If you love me, you will keep my commandments." Obedience is a way of showing our love for God and our trust in Him. It is also a way of demonstrating our faith in action. When we obey God, we experience the blessings that come from following His will, and we grow in our relationship with Him.

Keeping it real with God also means being authentic in our relationships with others. We should treat others with love, kindness, and respect, just as we would want to be treated ourselves. We should not be hypocritical or judgmental but should show compassion and forgiveness to those who have wronged us. We should also be willing to speak the truth in love, even when it is difficult.

In Matthew 18:15-17, Jesus gives us a clear example of how to deal with conflict in a way that honors God and keeps it real with others: "If another member of the church sins against you, go and point out the fault when the two of you are alone. If the member listens to you, you have regained that one. But if you are not listened to, take one or two others along with you, so that every word may be confirmed by the evidence of two or three witnesses. If the member refuses to listen to them, tell it to the church; and if the offender refuses to listen even to the church, let such a one be to you as a Gentile and a tax collector."

This passage teaches us the importance of confronting sin in a loving and truthful way, and of seeking reconciliation with our brothers and sisters in Christ.

In conclusion, keeping it real with God means living a life that is authentic and genuine, one that is based on our love for God and our love for others. It means being honest with ourselves and with Him about our sins and our need for His forgiveness. It means spending time in prayer, reading the Bible, and being obedient to His commands. It also means being authentic in our relationships with others, treating them with love, kindness, and respect, and confronting sin in a loving and truthful way. When we keep it real with God, we experience the fullness of His love and grace, and we are able to live a life that is pleasing to Him.

Prayer:

MOMENTS OF THOUGHTS DURING MY CHRISTIAN WALK

Heavenly Father,

As we embark on Chapter 9: "Keeping it real with God," we humbly come before You, acknowledging Your sovereignty and Your grace. In a world where standards often stray from Your truth, help us to keep it real with You by aligning our lives with Your Word and Your will.

Lord, forgive us for the times when we have blurred the line between Your way and the world's way, calling evil good and good evil. Grant us discernment to recognize moral distinctions and the courage to stand firm in Your truth, even when it goes against the tide of popular opinion.

Teach us, O Lord, to love You with all our heart, soul, and mind, and to love our neighbors as ourselves. May our lives be a testament to Your grace and mercy, reflecting Your love for those around us. Help us to be patient, kind, and compassionate, bearing with one another in love and seeking reconciliation when conflicts arise.

Lord, in our journey of faith, keep us humble and authentic in our worship and in our relationship with You. May we approach You with sincerity, pouring out our hearts in prayer and worship, and listening attentively for Your voice. Guide us in obedience to Your commands, knowing that true love for You is expressed through our actions.

Father, help us confront sin in a spirit of love and truth, seeking restoration and reconciliation in our relationships. Grant us the wisdom to address conflicts with humility and grace, following Jesus Christ's example.

Lord, we confess our sins and our need for Your forgiveness. Cleanse us from all unrighteousness and renew a right spirit within us. Help us to walk in the freedom and joy that come from knowing we are forgiven and loved by You.

In conclusion, Lord, help us to keep it real with You by living lives that are authentic and genuine, rooted in Your love and truth. May we experience the fullness of Your love and grace as we seek to honor You in all that we do.

We pray this in the name of Jesus Christ, our Lord and Savior.
Amen.

Chapter 10: Planned Out Evil

The story of Amnon and Tamar in 2 Samuel 13:1-22 is a tragic tale of a brother's evil desire for his sister and the devastating consequences that followed. This story serves as a warning against the dangers of lust and the evil that can arise from the planning and execution of wicked intentions.

Point 1: Plan

Amnon's desire for Tamar consumed him to the point of making himself ill. His advisor, Jonadab, suggested a plan for Amnon to lure Tamar to his bedroom under the guise of needing food. Amnon followed the plan and pretended to be sick when his father visited him, asking for Tamar to come and make him food. Tamar complied, and Amnon took the opportunity to grab and rape her.

This plan was carefully crafted to fulfill Amnon's lustful desires, and it shows the danger of planning for evil intentions. When we allow our desires to take control of us, we can become blind to the wickedness of our actions and justify them through the careful planning and execution of our plans.

Point 2: Action

Amnon's action in carrying out the plan was a heinous act of sexual assault and abuse of power. He ignored Tamar's pleas and went through with the rape, causing her immense pain and trauma. His actions were not only sinful but also illegal, and they violated God's commandments and the laws of the land.

Amnon's actions show the danger of acting on our wicked desires, even if we have planned for them. We must always resist evil and follow God's commands, no matter how strong our urges may be.

Point 3: Result

The result of Amnon's plan and action was devastating. Tamar was left desolate, shamed, and traumatized, and Amnon's hatred for her grew after the assault. Absalom, Tamar's brother, was also filled with rage and eventually murdered Amnon in revenge, leading to a cycle of violence and chaos in David's family.

The result of our evil plans and actions can have far-reaching consequences beyond our control. We must be mindful of the harm we can cause to others and the ripple effect of our actions.

The story of Amnon and Tamar is a cautionary tale of the dangers of lust, planning for evil, and acting on wicked desires. It shows the devastating consequences of sin and the importance of following God's commands and resisting temptation.

As we navigate through life, we must be vigilant against our sinful desires and avoid planning for evil. We must strive to follow God's commands and resist the temptations of the flesh, knowing that our actions have consequences beyond ourselves. May we always seek to do good, resist evil, and glorify God in all that we do.

Prayer:

MOMENTS OF THOUGHTS DURING MY CHRISTIAN WALK

Heavenly Father,

As we delve into Chapter 10: "Planned Out Evil," we come before You with humble hearts, recognizing the sobering lessons found in the story of Amnon and Tamar. Lord, we acknowledge the dangers of allowing sinful desires to consume us and the devastating consequences that can arise from planning and acting on wicked intentions.

Father, help us to guard our hearts against the allure of sinful desires that seek to lead us astray. Grant us wisdom and discernment to recognize the subtle ways in which evil can take root in our thoughts and intentions. May we be vigilant in resisting temptation and steadfast in our commitment to follow Your commands.

Lord, we pray for strength to resist the temptation to plan for evil, knowing that the consequences of such actions can be far-reaching and destructive. Help us to walk in the light of Your truth and to live lives that honor and glorify You in all that we do.

Father, we lift up those who have been victims of evil plans and actions, like Tamar in the story of Amnon. Comfort them in their pain and heal their wounds, both physical and emotional. Bring restoration and redemption to their lives, Lord, and help them to find healing and wholeness in Your presence.

We also pray for those who are tempted to carry out evil plans, like Amnon. Soften their hearts, Lord, and convict them of the wickedness of their intentions. Lead them to repentance and forgiveness, Father, and guide them onto the path of righteousness and obedience to Your will.

Lord, in a world where evil seems to lurk at every corner, help us to be beacons of Your light and agents of Your love. Empower us to stand firm against the schemes of the enemy and to overcome evil with good. May our lives be a testament to Your grace and mercy, shining brightly in the darkness and pointing others towards Your saving love.

We pray all these things in the name of Jesus Christ, our

Lord and Savior.

Amen.

Chapter 11: God Called You

God has a plan for each one of us. He has called us to fulfill a purpose in this world, to make a difference in the lives of those around us, and to leave a lasting impact on His kingdom. The story of Abram, later known as Abraham, is a powerful example of how God can call us to something great and lead us on a journey of faith and obedience. In Genesis 12:1-4, God tells Abram to leave his country, his relatives, and his father's house to go to a land that God will show him. God promises to make him a great nation, to bless him, and to bless all the families of the earth through him. This chapter will explore the themes of family and drama in the lives of Abram and his nephew Lot, and how their experiences can teach us about the importance of our own commitments, decisions, and actions as we strive to fulfill God's calling on our lives.

Point 1: Family
The story of Abram begins with his family. In Genesis 11:27-32, we learn that Abram's father, Terah, became the

father of Abram, Nahor, and Haran. Haran became the father of Lot, who would later accompany Abram on his journey. When Terah and his family left Ur of the Chaldeans to enter the land of Canaan, they settled in Haran. It was here that God called Abram to leave his father's house and go to a land that God would show him. Abram was obedient to God's call, taking his wife Sarai and his nephew Lot with him. God promised to make Abram a great nation, to bless him, and to bless all the families of the earth through him.

The story of Abram and his family teaches us about the importance of our own families. Our families play a significant role in shaping who we are and what we become. They can provide a foundation of support and encouragement as we navigate life's challenges and pursue our dreams. As Christians, we are called to honor and cherish our families, to love them unconditionally, and to seek God's guidance in our relationships with them. Like Abram, we may be called to leave our families to follow God's plan for our lives. However, we can trust that God will provide for us and lead us on a journey of faith and obedience.

Point 2: Drama

The story of Lot, Abram's nephew, is a tragic one. Lot lived in Sodom, a city known for its wickedness and immorality. Despite the warnings of impending judgment, Lot was reluctant to leave the city and had to be dragged out by the angels sent by God. Lot's wife looked back and was turned into a pillar of salt. Lot's two daughters survived with him, but they believed that they were the only ones left on earth and resorted to incest to preserve their family line.

The story of Lot teaches us about the dangers of making unwise decisions and the consequences that can follow. Lot's decision to live in Sodom was unwise, and he paid a high price for it. He lost his wife, and his family was destroyed by his daughters' actions. We must be careful to make wise decisions and to seek God's guidance in all that we do. We cannot afford to be complacent or to compromise our values for the sake of comfort or convenience. As Christians, we are called to live a life of integrity and to be a light in the darkness. We must stand firm in our faith and resist the temptations of the world around us.

God has called each one of us to fulfill a purpose in this world. He has given us unique gifts and talents that we can use to make a difference in the lives of those around us.

However, fulfilling God's calling in our lives is not always easy. We will face challenges, obstacles, and setbacks along the way. We will be tempted to take shortcuts, to compromise our values, and to give up when the going gets tough. But we must remember that God is with us every step of the way. He will guide us, strengthen us, and empower us to overcome any obstacle that we may face.

The stories of Abram and Lot remind us that our commitments, decisions, and actions significantly impact our lives and the lives of those around us. We must be intentional in our choices and seek God's guidance in all that we do. We must be willing to step out in faith, even when the path ahead is uncertain. We must trust in God's promises and believe that He will fulfill His plans for our lives.

For those of us who have made mistakes or bad decisions in the past, we must remember that nothing is irredeemable with our God. God is a God of second chances, and He can turn our mistakes into opportunities for growth and transformation. We may have to live with the consequences of our past decisions, but God can use even our failures to shape us into the person He has called us to be.

In conclusion, God has called each one of us to fulfill a purpose in this world. He has given us unique gifts and talents that we can use to make a difference in the lives of those around us. Like Abram and Lot, we will face challenges and obstacles along the way. But we can trust that God is with us every step of the way, guiding us, strengthening us, and empowering us to fulfill His calling on our lives. We must be intentional in our commitments, decisions, and actions, seeking God's guidance in all that we do. And we must remember that even our mistakes and failures can be redeemed by God's grace, shaping us into the person He has called us to be.

Prayer:

Heavenly Father,

As we reflect on Chapter 11: "God Called You," we come before You with hearts open to receive Your guidance and wisdom. We recognize the profound significance of Your call in our lives and the journey of faith and obedience that it entails. Lord, we look to the story of Abram, later known as Abraham, and his nephew Lot as powerful examples of Your calling and the challenges that accompany it.

Father, we thank You for the reminder that You have a purpose for each one of us. You have called us to make a difference in this world, to leave a lasting impact for Your kingdom. Help us to discern Your calling in our lives and to respond with faith and obedience, just as Abram did when You called him to leave his country and go to a land that You would show him.

Lord, we lift up our families to You. Like Abram, may we cherish and honor our families, recognizing the vital role they play in shaping who we are. Grant us the wisdom to navigate the complexities of family dynamics and the strength to prioritize our commitment to You above all else. Help us to trust You even when Your call leads us away from our families, knowing that You will provide for us and guide us on our journey.

Father, we also acknowledge the dangers of making unwise decisions, as demonstrated in the story of Lot. Protect us from the lure of worldly pleasures and the temptation to compromise our values for the sake of comfort or convenience. Grant us discernment to recognize Your will and the courage to follow it, even when the path ahead is uncertain.

Lord, we surrender our lives to You and Your calling. Equip us with Your strength and wisdom as we strive to fulfill Your purpose for our lives. Help us to be intentional in our commitments, decisions, and actions, seeking Your guidance in all that we do. And when we falter or make mistakes along the way, remind us of Your boundless grace and Your ability to redeem even our failures for Your glory.

In conclusion, Lord, we thank You for the privilege of being called by You. May we embrace Your calling with humility and gratitude, trusting in Your faithfulness to lead us and fulfill Your plans for our lives. May our lives be a testimony to Your goodness and Your power to transform hearts and lives. We pray all these things in the name of Jesus Christ, our Lord.
Amen.

Chapter 12: New Beginnings

The concept of a new beginning is not new to the Bible. In the book of Isaiah, the children of Israel are in a period of exile, and God speaks to them through the prophet Isaiah, encouraging them to forget the former things and focus on the new thing that He is about to do. This message of hope is just as relevant today as it was thousands of years ago. We all have things in our past that we would rather forget, and we all have areas in our lives where we could use a new beginning. This chapter will explore how we can embrace the new things that God wants to do in our lives and move forward into a brighter future.

Change Your Focus - Quit Looking Behind, Start Looking Ahead The first step to embracing the new thing that God wants to do in our lives is to change our focus. We need to stop dwelling on the past and start looking ahead to the future. The Bible says in Isaiah 43:18, "Forget the former things; do not dwell on the past." This is easier said than done, especially if we have experienced a lot of pain and hurt in the past. However, if we keep looking back at what has already happened, we will miss out on the new things that God wants to do in our lives.

Point 1: Exile

The concept of exile is a recurring theme in the Bible. It refers to a broken relationship between God and His people, where sin has separated them from Him. In the case of the children of Israel, they were in exile because of their disobedience and rebellion against God. However, God did not abandon them in their exile. Instead, He promised to make a way for them in the wilderness and streams in the wasteland (Isaiah 43:19). This promise of a new beginning was a message of hope to the people who had lost everything they had known and loved.

The same message of hope applies to us today. No matter how far we have strayed from God, He is always willing to make a way for us to come back to Him. We may feel like we are in a wilderness, with no hope of escape, but God is always working behind the scenes to make a way for us. We need to trust Him and believe that He will lead us to a new beginning.

You Cannot Depend Upon Past Victories to Sustain You

Another reason why we need to forget the former things is that we cannot depend upon past victories to sustain us. The children of Israel had experienced many victories in the past, such as leaving Egypt and conquering the land of Canaan. However, those victories did not help them in their current situation. They needed a new work, a new miracle, a new victory.

The same is true for us. We cannot rely on past successes to sustain us in the present. We need to keep moving forward and trusting God for new victories. Our past accomplishments can be a source of encouragement, but they should not be a crutch that we lean on when times get tough.

Point 2: Exodus

The concept of the Exodus is another example of God providing a new beginning for His people. The children of Israel were in bondage in Egypt, and God raised Moses to lead them out of slavery and into freedom. The Exodus was a powerful demonstration of God's power and faithfulness, and it provided a foundation for the children of Israel's faith.

In the same way, God wants to lead us out of our bondage and into freedom. We may feel stuck in a situation that we cannot escape from, but God is always working to provide a way out. We need to trust Him and follow His lead, even when it seems like there is no way forward.

You Cannot Allow Your Past Failures to Possess You

The children of Israel also had a history of failure and disobedience. They turned away from God and worshiped idols, even after He had blessed them with so much. However, God did not give up on them. He continued to love them and offer them a way back to Him.

Likewise, we cannot allow our past failures to possess us. We may have made mistakes and turned away from God in the past, but that does not mean that we cannot have a new beginning. God is always willing to forgive us and offer us a fresh start. We need to let go of our past mistakes and embrace the new things that God wants to do in our lives.

In conclusion, a new beginning is possible for all of us, no matter what our past may look like. We need to change our focus from the past to the future, trust God to make a way for us, and let go of our past failures. As the Bible says in 2 Corinthians 5:17, "Therefore, if anyone is in Christ, the new creation has come: The old has gone, the new is here!"

When we embrace God's new plan for our lives, we can move forward into a brighter future filled with hope and possibility. As we let go of the past and focus on the future, we can trust that God will guide us and provide for us every step of the way. With Him, we can do all things (Philippians 4:13).

Prayer:

Heavenly Father,

MOMENTS OF THOUGHTS DURING MY CHRISTIAN WALK

As we delve into Chapter 12: "New Beginning," we come before You with hearts open to Your transforming power and grace. Lord, we recognize the significance of Your promise of a new beginning in our lives, and we desire to embrace it fully.

Father, help us to change our focus from dwelling on the past to looking ahead to the future with hope and anticipation. Just as You instructed the children of Israel through Isaiah to forget the former things and embrace the new thing You were about to do, may we also release the burdens of our past and trust in Your promise of renewal and restoration.

Lord, we acknowledge that our past victories cannot sustain us in the present. Grant us the wisdom to understand that while our past accomplishments may serve as encouragement, our dependence must always be on You for new victories and breakthroughs. Help us to keep moving forward in faith, knowing that You are always leading us toward greater things.

Father, we are reminded of the Exodus, where You led Your people out of bondage and into freedom. Just as You provided a way out for the children of Israel, we trust that You will lead us out of any situation that holds us captive. Strengthen our faith to follow Your lead, even when the path forward seems uncertain.

Lord, we confess that we have allowed our past failures to hold power over us, but we know that in Christ, we are made new. Help us to release the grip of our past mistakes and embrace the forgiveness and grace You offer us. May we step boldly into the new beginning You have prepared for us, knowing that You are always with us, guiding us along the way.

In conclusion, Lord, we thank You for the promise of a new beginning. May we embrace it wholeheartedly, trusting in Your faithfulness and provision for our lives. Help us to let go of the past and focus on the future You have planned for us, filled with hope and possibility. With You, Lord, we can do all things, and we place our trust in Your unfailing love.

In Jesus' name, we pray.

Amen.

Chapter 13: Discipleship

Let me discuss Jude 1:4 and the warning it provides about false teachers who have slipped into the church and are perverting God's grace. In this chapter, we will focus on the importance of discipleship and how having a heart for God and submitting to Him can help us become effective disciples.

Point 1: Having A Heart For God
One of the key aspects of discipleship is having a heart for God. In Acts, we see that God chose David to replace Saul as king because David was a man after God's own heart. This means that David had a deep desire to know and follow God, and he was willing to obey Him even when it was difficult.

As Christians, we should also have a heart for God. This means that we should have a strong desire to know Him and follow His ways. We should seek to obey Him even when it goes against our own desires or the desires of others.

However, having a heart for God does not come naturally to us. We need to actively cultivate it by spending time in prayer, reading the Bible, and seeking to obey God's commands. When we do this, we will begin to see our hearts align more closely with God's, and we will become better disciples as a result.

Point 2: Submitting To God
Another important aspect of discipleship is submitting to God. In Romans 6, Paul reminds us that when we become followers of Christ, we are baptized into His death and raised to new life. This means that we are no longer slaves to sin, but we are free to live a new life in Christ.

However, this new life requires us to submit to God and resist the temptations of the world. As James 4:7 reminds us, we are to submit ourselves to God and resist the devil. When we do this, the devil will flee from us, and we will strengthen our faith.

Submitting to God also means being willing to do His will,

even when it is difficult or inconvenient. This may mean forgiving those who have hurt us, loving our enemies, or sharing our faith with others. When we submit to God in this way, we become better disciples and are able to fulfill the mission that God has given us.

In conclusion, discipleship is an essential part of the Christian life, and having a heart for God and submitting to Him are key components of effective discipleship. By cultivating a heart for God and submitting to His will, we can become better examples of Christ to the world around us. As Jesus said in Matthew 5:14-16, we are the light of the world, and we should let our light shine before others so that they may see our good works and glorify God. Let us strive to be effective disciples of Christ, and let us seek to bring glory to God in all that we do.

Expanding on this further, effective discipleship requires us to not only have a heart for God and submit to Him but also to actively engage in spiritual disciplines. These disciplines include prayer, Bible study, fellowship with other believers, and evangelism.

Prayer is a vital part of our relationship with God. It is through prayer that we can communicate with Him, seek His guidance, and ask for His help. As we spend time in prayer, we will develop a deeper understanding of God's will for our lives and grow in our faith.

Bible study is also essential to effective discipleship. The Bible is the foundation of our faith, and as we study it, we will gain a deeper understanding of who God is and what He desires for us. Through the study of Scripture, we can learn to discern truth from falsehood and grow in our knowledge of God's character and His plan for our lives.

Fellowship with other believers is also important in discipleship. As we gather, we can encourage and support one another, share our struggles and victories, and hold each other accountable. Fellowship also provides opportunities for us to use our gifts and talents to serve others and further God's kingdom.

Finally, evangelism is a crucial aspect of effective discipleship. Jesus' final command to His disciples was to go and make disciples of all nations (Matthew 28:19-20).

MOMENTS OF THOUGHTS DURING MY CHRISTIAN WALK

As followers of Christ, it is our responsibility to share the Gospel with those around us and lead them to a personal relationship with Jesus. This requires us to step out of our comfort zones, be willing to share our faith and demonstrate Christ's love to those who are lost and hurting.

In conclusion, effective discipleship requires a heart for God, submission to His will, engagement in spiritual disciplines, and a commitment to evangelism. As we strive to become better disciples of Christ, let us remember that it is only through God's grace and power that we can live a life that brings glory to Him. Let us continue to seek His guidance, follow His commands, and share the love of Christ with those around us.

Prayer:

Heavenly Father,

As we delve into Chapter 13: "Discipleship," we come before You with hearts open to Your teachings and guidance. Lord, we recognize the importance of discipleship in our journey of faith and the role it plays in shaping us into effective ambassadors for Your kingdom.

Father, we acknowledge the warning in Jude 1:4 about false teachers who pervert Your grace. In a world filled with deception and distractions, we seek Your wisdom to discern truth from falsehood and to remain steadfast in our commitment to You.

Lord, help us cultivate a heart for You, just as David was a man after Your own heart. Grant us a deep desire to know You intimately and to follow Your ways wholeheartedly. May our lives be characterized by obedience to Your commands, even when it's difficult or unpopular.

Father, we understand the importance of submitting to You and resisting the temptations of the world. Empower us to live victoriously in Christ, knowing that we are no longer slaves to sin but free to live a new life in Him. Strengthen us to resist the schemes of the enemy and to walk in Your truth.

Lord, as we engage in spiritual disciplines like prayer,

Bible study, fellowship, and evangelism, may Your Holy Spirit guide and empower us. Help us to be diligent in our pursuit of You, seeking Your face in prayer and immersing ourselves in Your Word. Lead us to meaningful fellowship with other believers, where we can encourage, support, and grow together in faith. And embolden us to share the Gospel with those who need to hear it, demonstrating Your love and grace in all that we do.

In conclusion, Lord, we thank You for the privilege of discipleship and the opportunity to be Your ambassadors in the world. May our hearts be aligned with Yours, our lives be submitted to Your will, and our actions reflect Your love and truth. Guide us, Lord, as we strive to become better disciples of Christ, bringing glory to Your name in all that we do.

In Jesus' name, we pray.
Amen.

Chapter 14: Letting Sin Stop Your Growth and Decisions

As Christians, we all fall short of the glory of God. We struggle with sin and its consequences on a daily basis. This struggle can be exhausting and frustrating, especially when we try to overcome it on our own strength. The apostle Paul, a disciple of Christ, also struggled with sin. In Romans 7:18-20, he admits, "For I know that nothing good dwells in me, that is, in my flesh; for the willing is present in me, but the doing of the good is not. For the good that I want, I do not do, but I practice the very evil that I do not want. But if I am doing the very thing I do not want, I am no longer the one doing it, but sin which dwells in me." In this chapter, we will explore how letting sin stop your growth and decisions can be detrimental to your spiritual life and how to overcome it.

Point 1: God Is Stronger Than Our Struggles
Paul's struggle with sin is a clear indication that even the most devout Christians are not immune to its power. In

Romans 7:15, he expresses his frustration, "I do not understand what I do. For what I want to do, I do not do, but what I hate I do." The battle between our flesh and our spirit is real, and it can be overwhelming.

However, the good news is that God is stronger than our struggles. In Romans 7:24-25, Paul asks, "What a wretched man I am! Who will rescue me from this body that is subject to death? Thanks be to God, who delivers me through Jesus Christ our Lord!" Jesus Christ has already won the victory over sin and death. We need to surrender our struggles to Him and ask for His help. He is always ready to help us overcome our weaknesses.

Point 2: Put On The Full Armor
Ephesians 6:14-17 teaches us how to put on the full armor of God. This armor protects us from the attacks of the enemy, including the temptations of sin. We need to stand firm with the belt of truth buckled around our waist, the breastplate of righteousness in place, and our feet fitted with the readiness that comes from the gospel of peace. We also need to take up the shield of faith, with which we

can extinguish all the flaming arrows of the evil one. We need the helmet of salvation and the sword of the Spirit, which is the word of God.

Putting on the full armor of God is not a one-time event. It is a daily practice that we need to make a habit. Every day, we need to consciously put on the armor of God, pray for protection, and meditate on His word. We need to be vigilant and ready to defend ourselves against the attacks of the enemy.

Romans 12:2 teaches us to renew our minds. We need to start looking at things in a different light, with a renewed perspective. We need to stop conforming to the patterns of this world and be transformed by the renewing of our minds. We need to demolish arguments and every pretension that sets itself up against the knowledge of God and take captive every thought to make it obedient to Christ.

We also need to get a daily dose of God. We need to spend time in prayer, meditation, and studying His word. We need to walk in the Spirit and allow Him to guide us. We need to be intentional about our spiritual growth and make it a priority.

In conclusion, letting sin stop your growth and decisions can be detrimental to your spiritual life. However, God is stronger than our struggles, and we can overcome sin through Him. We need to put on the full armor of God daily, be vigilant, and be ready to defend ourselves against the attacks of the enemy. We also need to renew our minds, stop conforming to the patterns of this world, and get a daily dose of God.

As we continue to walk in faith, we will face challenges and temptations. We may stumble and fall, but we need to remember that God is always with us. He will never leave us nor forsake us. We need to trust in Him and rely on His strength to overcome sin and grow spiritually.

Letting sin stop your growth and decisions is a choice that we make. We can either give in to sin and its consequences or choose to follow God and His ways. The choice is ours. As Paul said in Romans 7:25, "So then, I myself in my mind am a slave to God's law, but in my sinful nature a slave to the law of sin." We need to choose whom we will serve and obey.

In conclusion, we must recognize our struggles with sin and not let it stop our growth and decisions. God is stronger than our struggles, and we can overcome sin through Him. We need to put on the full armor of God, renew our minds, and get a daily dose of God. Let us choose to follow God and His ways, and He will guide us on the path of righteousness.

Chapter 15: The Word Love Will Make You Think You Are Doing Right

Love is a powerful and complex emotion that can lead us to do great things for those we care about. However, it can also blind us and cause us to make decisions that are not truly in our best interest. The Bible warns us about this in Proverbs 14:12, where it says, "There is a way that appears to be right, but in the end it leads to death." In this chapter, we will explore the idea that the word love can make us think we are doing the right thing, but it is important to examine our motivations and actions to ensure that we are truly doing what is morally good, justified, and acceptable.

Point 1: Lowering Standards

One danger of the word love is that it can lead us to lower our standards and accept behaviors or actions that are not in line with our values or morals. For example, a parent may love their child so much that they refuse to hold them accountable for their actions, even when they are clearly in the wrong. This can create a situation where the child does not learn to take responsibility for their actions and may continue to engage in harmful behaviors. In Romans 6:21, it says, "What benefit did you reap at that time from the things you are now ashamed of? Those things result in death!" This passage reminds us that our actions have consequences, and just because something feels good at the moment does not mean it is the right thing to do. We must be willing to hold ourselves and others accountable to a higher standard, even if it is difficult or uncomfortable.

Point 2: Not Thinking Of Conscience

Another danger of the word love is that it can cause us to ignore our conscience and make decisions that we know are not right. Proverbs 12:15 says, "The way of fools seems right to them, but the wise listen to advice." This passage reminds us that just because something seems right to us does not mean it is the best course of action.

For example, a person may be in an unhealthy or abusive relationship, but they convince themselves that they are staying because they love their partner. In reality, they may be ignoring the inner voice that is telling them to leave and prioritizing their partner's needs over their own well-being. It is important to listen to our conscience and seek advice from wise and trusted sources when we are unsure of the right thing to do.

In order to truly do what is right, we must trust in the Lord and seek His guidance in all areas of our lives. Proverbs 3:5 says, "Trust in the LORD with all your heart and lean not on your own understanding." This passage reminds us that we cannot rely solely on our own wisdom and understanding, but must instead turn to God for direction and guidance.

Furthermore, Deuteronomy 6:5 says, "You shall love the LORD your God with all your heart and with all your soul and with all your might." This passage reminds us that our love for God should be the foundation of our actions and decisions. When we prioritize our love for God above all else, we are more likely to make decisions that align with His will and are truly morally good, justified, and acceptable.

In conclusion, the word love can be a powerful motivator, but it is important to examine our actions and decisions to ensure that they are truly in line with our values and morals. We must hold ourselves and others accountable to a higher standard and listen to our conscience when we are unsure of the right course of action. Above all, we must trust in the Lord and prioritize our love for Him above all else, knowing that He will guide us to the right decision.

Chapter 16: Sin Has The Same Outcome

Sin is a reality that we all face, and it has been present in our world since the fall of man in the Garden of Eden. Sin is the reason why we need a savior, and it is the reason why Jesus Christ died on the cross. Despite its prevalence, many people today fail to understand the true nature and consequences of sin. The title of this chapter, "Sin has the same outcome," is taken from the book of Jeremiah, where the prophet warns that trusting in man and turning away from God leads to a life of spiritual drought and barrenness. In this chapter, we will explore the different consequences of sin and how it affects our relationship with God and others.

Point 1: Separation

The Bible teaches us that sin creates a separation between us and God. In Isaiah 59:2, we read, "But your iniquities (sin) have made a separation between you and your God." This separation is caused by the fact that God is holy, and sin is contrary to His nature. When we choose to sin, we are essentially telling God that we do not want to be in a relationship with Him. This separation can be felt in our lives when we stop hearing the voice of the Holy Spirit and lose our sense of spiritual direction. It can lead to a life of spiritual drought and barrenness, just as Jeremiah warned.

The good news is that God has made a way for us to bridge the gap between us and Him. Through the death and resurrection of Jesus Christ, we can be reconciled to God and have our sins forgiven. This is why repentance is such an essential part of the Christian life. When we repent of our sins and turn back to God, we can experience the joy and fulfillment that comes from being in a relationship with Him.

Point 2: Trusting Worldly People With Godly Decision

Another consequence of sin is that it can lead us to trust in worldly people instead of God. Micah 7:5-8 warns us not to put our trust in our neighbors, friends, or even those closest to us. When we do this, we are essentially saying that we trust in their wisdom and guidance more than we trust in God's. This can lead us down a path of destruction, as worldly people are not always guided by God's principles and values.

In contrast, when we put our trust in God, we can be assured that He will guide us in the right direction. Proverbs 3:5-6 says, "Trust in the Lord with all your heart and lean not on your own understanding; in all your ways submit to him, and he will make your paths straight." When we trust in God, we can have the confidence that He will guide us in the right direction and that His plans for us are good.

Point 3: It Is Harmful To You And Others

Finally, sin is harmful not just to us but also to others around us. When we choose to live in sin, it can have a ripple effect on those closest to us. King Herod's sin is a perfect example of this. Herod's selfish ambition and jealousy led him to order the massacre of innocent children. His sin had a devastating impact on the families of those children and on the community as a whole.

Similarly, our sin can impact those around us. It can cause

pain and hurt and even lead others astray. This is why it is so important for us as believers to live lives that honor God and are characterized by love, compassion, and forgiveness.

In conclusion, sin is a reality that we all face, and it has significant consequences. It creates a separation between us and God, leads us to trust in worldly people instead of God, and can be harmful to both us and those around us. However, the good news is that through repentance and faith in Jesus Christ, we can be reconciled to God and experience the joy and fulfillment that comes from being in a relationship with Him. We can also trust in God's guidance and wisdom instead of worldly people, and we can strive to live lives that honor God and bring blessings to those around us.

As believers, we must also be aware of the impact that our sin can have on others. We must strive to live lives characterized by love, compassion, and forgiveness and seek to bring healing and reconciliation to those who have been hurt by our sin.

Ultimately, we must remember that sin has the same

outcome - separation from God. We must be vigilant in our fight against sin and seek to live lives that are pleasing to God. As Paul writes in Romans 6:23, "For the wages of sin is death, but the gift of God is eternal life in Christ Jesus our Lord." Let us, therefore, strive to live lives that are characterized by repentance, faith, and obedience to God, so that we may experience the fullness of life that He has promised us.

Made in the USA
Middletown, DE
18 October 2024